C000264849

More Quips and Quotes

for preachers, teachers, speakers and editors

Collected by

H. J. RICHARDS

Kevin Mayhew

First published in 2000 by
KEVIN MAYHEW LTD
Buxhall
Stowmarket
Suffolk IP14 3BW

© 2000 H. J. Richards

The right of H. J. Richards to be identified as the author
of this work has been asserted by him in accordance with
the Copyright, Designs and Patents Act 1988.

All rights reserved. No part of this publication may be
reproduced, stored in a retrieval system, or transmitted,
in any form or by any means, electronic, mechanical,
photocopying, recording or otherwise, without the
prior written permission of the publisher.

0 1 2 3 4 5 6 7 8 9

ISBN 1 84003 667 2
Catalogue No 1500404

Cover design by Jonathan Stroulger
Typesetting by Margaret Lambeth
Printed and bound in Great Britain

FOREWORD

I don't know when, or even why, I began to become a life-long magpie, hoarding things for a rainy day. Most children in my day collected cigarette cards and stamps. But from a very early age I was on to tram tickets, wine labels, beer mats, serviettes, theatre programmes and foreign coins. As I grew up I became more sophisticated, and started to collect epigrams, shrewd observations and witticisms, largely to enliven many a page of an otherwise dull lecture: they kept the students awake.

I published a selection of 500 or so of these in 1997. The warm response has encouraged me to dig into my dog-eared exercise books for a further selection. They are as haphazard as my reading has been over the years, but my detailed index may help teachers, speakers and preachers to find the *bon mot* that will hit off the point they are trying to make. As for myself, I join hands with the essayist who signed off his last volume with the words:

> I have done nothing more in this book than collect together the flowers which others have picked. All I have contributed is the ribbon to tie them into a bouquet.
>
> *Montaigne (1533-1592)*

H. J. RICHARDS

1

An anthology is like all the plums and orange peel picked out of a cake.

Walter Raleigh (1861-1922)

2

Nothing so divides Christians as their lust for unity.

3

Instruction issued to Sir Ronald Storrs, British Governor of Palestine in 1917: 'I hear very bad things about you from both the Jews and the Arabs. If either of them stops, you are out of a job.'

David Lloyd-George (1863-1945)

4

Nothing may be changed that would disagree with this (Latin Vulgate) edition of the Bible; not a single paragraph, not a single sentence, not a single word, not a single syllable, not a single iota.

Leon de Castro, Spanish Inquisitor, 1576

5

You can get much further with a kind word and a gun than you can with a kind word alone.

Al Capone (1899-1947)

6

Changing denominations is like swapping cabins on the *Titanic*.

Dominic Kirkham, O.Praem.

7

When Janet Street Porter sold off her wardrobe in 1997, Cable Television commented: 'She has done for fashion what the M25 has done for hedgehogs.'

8

Definition of a lie: An abomination to the Lord, but a very present help in time of trouble.

9

I don't like the family Stein!
There is Gert, there is Ep, there is Ein.
Gert's writings are punk,
Ep's statues are junk,
And no one can understand Ein.

Anon, 1920s

10

There is nothing to it. You only have to hit the right notes at the right time, and the organ plays itself.

Johann Sebastian Bach (1685-1750)

11

Asked 'What is sin?', the Buddhist monk replied:
'What can you do with your two hands open?'
'Arrange flowers, work, embrace, feed, and so on.'
'Now close them. What can you do with your two fists?'
'Hit, hurt, injure, perhaps kill.'
'That is what sin is.'

12

Disneyland embodies the Disney Corporation's idea of what the world ought to be like. After just a few hours inside, you begin to understand why the USA produces so many homicidal maniacs.

N. Middleton, 1997

13

Both the British and the Germans love France, but would rather that the French didn't live there.

14

As shadow Home Secretary, I kept waking up to the *Today* programme to hear of Home Office decisions I knew nothing about. Now that I'm Home Secretary, it's exactly the same.

Jack Straw, b. 1946

15

If you ask a Dane, 'Do you speak English?', he will reply, 'No, not very well. But now I will tell you the story of my life.' If you ask a Frenchman the same question, he will reply, 'Yes, but I am not going to.'

16

A voice from a Bethlehem stable on January 6, AD 1: 'I dunno. You wait a lifetime for a wise man to show up, and then three come all at once.'

17

The height of the great pyramid of Cheops (147 metres) is exactly one billionth of the distance between the earth and the sun.

18

By identifying the new learning with heresy, you make orthodoxy synonymous with ignorance.

Erasmus (1466-1536)

19

Oxford is on the whole more attractive than Cambridge to the ordinary visitor; and the traveller is therefore recommended to visit Cambridge first, or to omit it altogether if he cannot visit both.

Baedeker's Guide, 1887

20

How do I know that I'm God? Simple. I start praying and find I'm talking to myself.

Earl of Gurney, in Peter Barnes' (b. 1931) 'The Ruling Class'

21

The only thing I learnt at the BBC was how to yawn without opening my mouth.

Denis Norden (b. 1922)

22

When a lady told Whistler (1834-1903) that she knew only two painters in the world, himself and Velasquez, he replied, 'Why drag in Velasquez?'

23

Derek Nimmo's wife, wearing a fur coat, was accosted by an animal rights protester: 'What wretched creature had to die to let you wear that?' She replied, 'My mother-in-law.'

24

It is a revealed truth (*see* Luke 17:7-10) that slaves may be bought, sold, exchanged or given away.

Holy Office Decree 1866, signed by Pope Pius IX

25

We should always be aware that our Christian creeds are only the result of a majority vote at a meeting.

Dean Inge (1860-1954)

26

Faith makes many of the mountains which it has to remove.

Dean Inge (1860-1954)

27

The plaque put up in St Paul's, London, in honour of the architect Christopher Wren reads, *Si monumentum requiris, circumspice* – 'If you're looking for a monument, look around you.' With the increasing traffic on Ludgate Hill in the '50s, and '60s, Dean Inge suggested it should now read, 'If you're *not* looking for a monument, look around you.'

28

When I came back to Dublin, I was courtmartialled in my absence and sentenced to death in my absence, so I said they could shoot me in my absence.

Brendan Behan (1923-1964)

29

Strong brother in God and last companion, Wine.

Hilaire Belloc (1870-1953)

30

I am a sundial and I make a botch
of what is done much better by a watch.

Hilaire Belloc (1870-1953)

31

The jury system consists of asking the ignorant to use the incomprehensible to decide the unknowable.

US Judge Zobel (b. 1932)

32

By night an atheist half believes in God.

Edward Young (1683-1765)

33

Christians are those who feel repentance on a Sunday for what they did on Saturday and will continue to do on Monday.

34

I read the book of Job last night. I don't think God comes well out of it.

Virginia Woolf (1882-1941)

35

Three people may be able to keep a secret, if two of them are dead.

36

The highest praise of God consists in the denial of him by the atheist who finds creation so perfect that it can dispense with a creator.

Marcel Proust (1871-1922)

37

Seen at the back of church, a bowl marked 'For the Sick', with a second notice added later: 'This bowl is for monetary donations only.'

38

Definition of a bassoon: An ill wind that nobody blows good.

39

Money can't buy friends, but you get a better class of enemy.

Spike Milligan (b. 1918)

40

The worst of madmen is a saint run mad.

Alexander Pope (1688-1744)

41

Guidelines for bureaucrats:
a. When in charge, ponder.
b. When in trouble, delegate.
c. When in doubt, mumble.

James Boren (b. 1925)

42

You cannot hope to bribe or twist,
thank God! The British journalist.
But seeing what the man will do
unbribed, there's no occasion to.

Humbert Wolfe (1886-1940)

43

Growing old is like being increasingly penalised for a
crime you haven't committed.

Anthony Powell (1905-2000)

44

Apart from the known and the unknown, what else is
there?

Harold Pinter (b. 1930)

45

Evil will always exist, always at odds with the good. It can
find no place with God in heaven, only on earth. That is
why we should try to escape from earth to heaven as
quickly as we can.

Plato (429-347 BC)

46

The rain, it raineth on the just
And also on the unjust fella:
But chiefly on the just, because
The unjust steals the just's umbrella.

Lord Bowen (1835-1894)

47

Education makes a people easy to lead, but difficult to drive; easy to govern, but impossible to enslave.

Lord Brougham (1778-1868)

48

You can spend the whole of your life trying to be popular, but at the end of the day the size of the crowd at your funeral will be largely dictated by the weather.

Frank Skinner (b. 1957)

49

When Harold Macmillan's Chancellor Selwyn Lloyd was summarily sacked in 1962, he complained that even his cook would be given a week's notice of dismissal. 'Of course', Macmillan replied, 'but a good cook is much harder to replace than a Chancellor.'

50

An atheist is a man who has no invisible means of support.

John Buchan (1875-1940)

51

Thank God, I am still an atheist.

Luis Buñuel (1900-1983)

52

On being asked to condemn the works of Teilhard de Chardin, Pope Pius XII (1876-1958) said, 'One Galileo in two thousand years is enough.'

53

My soul, do not seek immortal life,
But exhaust the realm of the possible.

Pindar (518-438 BC)

54

No pain, no palm;
No thorns, no throne;
No gall, no glory;
No cross, no crown.

William Penn (1644-1718)

55

She fitted into my biggest armchair as if it had been built
round her by someone who knew they were wearing arm-
chairs tight about the hips that season.

P. G. Wodehouse (1881-1975)

56

It is a dangerous state to be in, thinking you understand.

Paul Valéry (1871-1945)

57

In a recent experiment, two mobile phones were laid
either side of a fresh egg, and the connection between them
dialled. After fifteen minutes the egg was hard-boiled.

58

At fifty, everyone has the face he deserves.

George Orwell (1903-1950)

59

Rome is the ideal mother. She has too many children and, being unable to take care of any of them, she doesn't ask anything of you. She welcomes you when you come, and lets you go when you leave.

Federico Fellini (b. 1920)

60

Bury me where you like, it doesn't matter. Nowhere is far away from God. Do you imagine that at the end of the world he won't know the place from which to raise me from the dead?

Monica, mother of St Augustine (332-387)

61

People lean on the boundary wall of the Roman Forum all day long, peering down into the ruins as if they expected something to happen; but nothing ever does, except perhaps a cat stalking a mouse through what was once the centre of the world.

H. V. Morton (1892-1979)

62

If these writings of the Greeks (in the library of Alexandria, burnt down in AD 641) agree with the Koran, they are useless and need not be preserved; if they disagree, they are pernicious and ought to be destroyed.

Caliph Omar (581-644)

63

Becoming a father is easy. What is difficult is being a father.

Wilhelm Busch (1832-1908)

64

Some have meat and cannot eat,
Some cannot eat that want it:
But we have meat and we can eat,
Sae let the Lord be thankit.

Robert Burns (1759-1796)

65

The Catholic Church has never really come to terms with women. What I object to is being treated either as Madonnas or Mary Magdalenes.

Shirley Williams (b. 1930)

66

I have been told that Wagner's music is better than it sounds.

Bill Nye (1850-1896)

67

Hickory, dickory, dock,
Two mice ran up the clock.
The clock struck one,
The other one got away.

68

When I want a peerage, I shall buy it like an honest man.

Alfred Harmsworth (1865-1922)

69

One would be in less danger
From the wiles of a stranger
If one's own kin and kith
Were more fun to be with.

Ogden Nash (1902-1971)

70

I test my bath before I sit,
And I'm always moved to wonderment
That what chills the finger not a bit
Is so frigid upon the fundament.

Ogden Nash (1902-1971)

71

We are all in the gutter, but some of us are looking at the stars.

Oscar Wilde (1854-1900)

72

Sir, the pretending to extraordinary revelations and gifts of the Holy Ghost is a horrid thing – a very horrid thing.

Joseph Butler (1692-1752) to John Wesley

73

The way God gives his grace is scandalous.

John Henry Newman (1801-1890)

74

When Pope John XXIII succeeded Pius XII in 1958, an observer summed up the general feeling with, '*Quel altro* (the other fellow) was closer to God, but *questo* (this fellow) is closer to us.'

75

Life is rather like a tin of sardines: we're all of us looking for the key.

Alan Bennett (b. 1934) in 'Beyond the Fringe'

76

We've all heard that a million monkeys banging on a million typewriters will eventually produce the entire works of Shakespeare. Now, thanks to the Internet, we know this is not true.

Robert Wilensky (b. 1951)

77

A cynic is a man who knows the price of everything and the value of nothing.

Oscar Wilde (1854-1900)

78

He (Anthony Eden) was not only a bore; he bored for England.

Malcolm Muggeridge (1903-1990)

79

If something good happens to you, be sure to tell your friends to make them feel bad.

Count Casimir (1768-1843)

80

English people are far too busy to be polite as well.

Montesquieu (1689-1755)

81

All this I could demonstrate by reason. Since you are an English audience, I will give you ten minutes of oratory, and convince you.

Hilaire Belloc (1870-1953)

82

An apology for the Devil: it must be remembered that we have only heard one side of the case. God has written all the books.

Samuel Butler (1835-1902)

83

It was very good of God to let Carlyle and Mrs Carlyle marry one another and so make only two people miserable instead of four.

Samuel Butler (1835-1902)

84

The Church only complains of persecution when it is not allowed to persecute.

Luis de Zulueta

85

People never do evil so cheerfully and so completely as when they do it out of religious conviction.

Pascal (1623-1662)

86

When Lord Soper (1903-1998) was asked how he always managed to remain so consistent, he replied, 'By ignoring some of the facts.'

87

Gilbert White, of Selborne, noted in his diary for 4 December 1770 that owls hoot in B flat, strictly at concert pitch.

88

When people cease to believe in something, they do not believe in nothing; they believe in anything.

G. K. Chesterton (1874-1936)

89

Religion is the wound, not the bandage.

Dennis Potter (1935-1994)

90

He (Dean Inge) was always bold, clear, concise, cultured, forceful, graceful, classical, eloquent, and wrong.

Ian Mackay

91

Even reason is a matter of faith. It is an act of faith to assert that our thoughts have any relationship to reality at all.

G. K. Chesterton (1874-1936)

92

The future is a time when the language of religion will be as useless as toy money.

Karl Marx (1818-1883)

93

Sometimes people ask if religion and science are opposed to each other. They are: in the sense that the thumb and fingers of my hand are opposed to one another. It is an opposition by means of which anything can be grasped.

Sir William Bragg (1890-1971)

94

Joan of Arc: I hear voices telling me what to do. They come from God.
Robert: They come from your imagination.
Joan of Arc: Of course. That is how the messages of God come to us.

George Bernard Shaw (1856-1950)

95

Now, Barabbas was a publisher.

Thomas Campbell (1777-1844)

96

The opposite of love is not hate, it's indifference.
The opposite of art is not ugliness, it's indifference.
The opposite of faith is not heresy, it's indifference.
And the opposite of life is not death, it's indifference.

Elie Wiesel (b. 1928)

97

Democracy is the recurrent suspicion that more than half of the people are right more than half of the time.

E. B. White (1899-1985)

98

A child is not a vase to be filled, but a fire to be lit.

François Rabelais (1494-1553)

99

A woman is like a teabag: only in hot water do you realise how strong she is.

Nancy Reagan (b. 1923)

100

Ask any man what nationality he would prefer to be, and ninety-nine out of a hundred will tell you that they would prefer to be Englishmen.

Cecil Rhodes (1853-1902)

101

Never cut what you can untie.

102

How do I know what I think until I hear what I say?

E. M. Forster (1879-1970)

103

It is not that the Englishman can't feel – it is that he is afraid to feel. He has been taught at his public school that feeling is bad form. He must not express great joy or sorrow, or even open his mouth too wide when he talks – his pipe might fall out if he did.

E. M. Forster (1879-1970)

104

I class myself as a moderate. I try to maintain that delicate balance between right and wrong.

Peter De Rosa (b. 1932)

105

An epitaph is a belated advertisement for a line of goods that has been permanently discontinued.

I. Cobb (b. 1944)

106

Nature doth paynt them (women) to be weak, fraile, impacient, feble, and foolishe; and experience hath declared tham to be unconstant, variable, cruell, and lacking the spirit of counsel and regiment.

John Knox (1505-1575)

107

I have to believe in the Apostolic Succession. There is no other way of explaining the descent of the Bishop of Exeter from Judas Iscariot.

Sydney Smith (1771-1845)

108

I don't object to the Old Man (Gladstone) always having the ace of trumps up his sleeve, but merely to his belief that God Almighty put it there.

Henry Labouchere (1831-1912)

109

Heckler: Go ahead, Al (Smith, 1873-1944). Tell 'em all you know. It won't take you long.
Al Smith: If I tell 'em all we both know, it won't take me any longer.

110

Always forgive your enemies – but never forget their names.

Robert F. Kennedy (1925-1968)

111

He is every other inch a gentleman.

Noel Coward (1899-1973)

112

Dr (John) Donne's verses are like the Peace of God: they pass all understanding.

King James I (1566-1625)

113

Moral indignation is jealousy with a halo.

H. G. Wells (1866-1946)

114

I don't know what effect these men will have upon the enemy, but, by God, they frighten me.

Duke of Wellington (1759-1862)

115

For years a secret shame destroyed my peace –
I'd not read Eliot, Auden or MacNeice.
But then I had a thought that brought me hope –
Neither had Chaucer, Shakespeare, Milton, Pope.

Justin Richardson (1900-1975)

116

The trouble with England is that there are sixty different religions, and only one sauce.

Francesco Caracciolo (1752-1799)

117

Orthodoxy is my doxy; heterodoxy is another man's doxy.

William Warburton (1698-1779)

118

Any man who hates dogs and babies can't be all bad.

Leo Rosten (1908-1997)

119

If I have seen further, it is by standing on the shoulders of giants.

Isaac Newton (1642-1727)

120

If everything else in this nation of ours were lost but cricket – her Constitution and the laws of England – it would be possible to reconstruct from the theory and practice of cricket all the eternal Englishness which has gone to the establishment of that Constitution and the laws.

Neville Cardus (1889-1975)

121

There are only two emotions in a plane: boredom and terror.

Orson Welles (1915-1985)

122

When he heard that Randolph Churchill's lung, when removed, proved to be non-malignant, Evelyn Waugh (1903-1966) called it 'a typical triumph of modern science – to find the only part of Randolph that was not malignant and remove it'.

123

Anyone who has been to an English public school will always feel comparatively at home in prison.

Evelyn Waugh (1903-1966)

124

When he was asked on his deathbed in 1778 to renounce the Devil, Voltaire replied, 'This is no time for making new enemies.'

125

The group of countries which were called, and still call themselves, the Holy Roman Empire, were neither holy, nor Roman, nor an empire.

Voltaire (1694-1778)

126

I long ago came to the conclusion that all life is 6 to 5 against.

Damon Runyon (1884-1946)

127

If Jesus Christ were to come today, people would not even crucify him. They would ask him to dinner, and hear what he had to say, and make fun of it.

Thomas Carlyle (1795-1881)

128

To steal from one author is called plagiarism. To steal from many is called research.

129

A little inaccuracy sometimes saves tons of explanation.

Saki (1870-1916)

130

A healthy male adult bore consumes each year one and a half times his own weight in other people's patience.

John Updike (b. 1932)

131

I am just going to pray for you at St Paul's, but with no very lively hope of success.

Sydney Smith (1771-1845)

132

God may well be loved, but not thought; by love he may be caught, but by thinking never.

Cloud of Unknowing (14th century)

133

If I could understand religion the way I understand that two plus two equals four, I wouldn't bother with it.

Friedrich von Hügel (1852-1925)

134

The only obligation to which in advance we may hold a novel, without incurring the accusation of being arbitrary, is that it be interesting.

Henry James (1843-1916)

135

The novel is practically a Protestant form of art: it is a product of the free mind, of the autonomous individual.

George Orwell (1903-1950)

136

God separated Britain from mainland Europe, and it was for a purpose.

Margaret Thatcher (b. 1925)

137

You know you're getting old when you stoop down to tie your shoelaces, and wonder what else you can do while you're down there.

138

A consumer society creates two kinds of slaves: the prisoners of addiction and the prisoners of envy.

Ivan Illich (b. 1926)

139

If thou wouldst see Melrose aright,
Go visit it by pale moonlight.
If thou wouldst see Melrose awrong,
Go visit it by charabong.

Beachcomber (1893-1979)

140

Puritanism is the haunting fear that someone, somewhere, may be happy.

H. L. Mencken (1880-1956)

141

I don't need people to support me when I'm in the right, only when I'm in the wrong.

Lord Melbourne (1779-1848)

142

In defeat unbeatable, in victory unbearable.

Winston Churchill (1874-1965) on General Montgomery

143

Golf is a very good walk ruined.

Mark Twain (1835-1910)

144

As a teacher, I like to think of myself as Jesus did – a shepherd caring for his sheep. Most of mine are only woolly on the inside.

Peter De Rosa (b. 1932)

145

He uses statistics as a drunken man uses a lamppost – for support rather than illumination.

Andrew Lang (1844-1912)

146

He who hesitates is probably right.

147

The prisoner due for execution has to state his wishes for the disposition of his body. He writes, 'I want it resuscitated.'

148

A truth that's told with bad intent
Beats all the lies you can invent.

William Blake (1757-1827)

149

Pope Gregory the Great (540-604) was so moved by the relief on Trajan's Column showing the emperor helping a woman whose son had been killed, that he begged God to release the emperor's soul from hell. God duly appeared to the pope in a vision, and assured him that Trajan had been rescued, but requested him not to pray for the souls of any more pagans.

150

At the height of the Battle of Waterloo (1815), Lord Uxbridge was told by the Duke of Wellington, 'By God, Sir, you've lost your leg.' He replied, 'By God, Sir, so I have.'

151

It (the Falklands War, 1982) was like two bald men fighting over a comb.

J. L. Borges (1899-1986)

152

When I was asked by Isaiah Berlin how anyone with a double first in philosophy at Cambridge could be a believer, I told him, 'If it makes it any easier for you, just think of me as a lapsed heretic.'

Rabbi Jonathan Sacks (b. 1948)

153

I know damn well what the public want, and they're not going to get it.

Lord Reith, Director-General of the BBC, 1927-1928

154

Life is doubt, and faith without doubt is nothing but death.

Miguel de Unamuno (1864-1937)

155

If at first you don't succeed, don't try skydiving.

156

I like pigs. Cats look down on you. Dogs look up to you. But pigs treat you as equals.

Winston Churchill (1874-1965)

157

Good news never comes in brown envelopes.

158

'If you could interview a person, living or dead, whom would you choose?'
'The living one.'

159

Jesus loved the aristocracy . . . He personally chose to be born of a noble line, and made his family tree known in the Gospels.

Pope Pius IX (1792-1878)

160

A critic is a man who knows the way but can't drive the car.

Kenneth Tynan (1927-1980)

161

Familiarity breeds contempt – and children.

Mark Twain (1835-1910)

162

When angry, count four; when very angry, swear.

Mark Twain (1835-1910)

163

English policy is to float lazily downstream, occasionally putting out a diplomatic boathook to avoid collisions.

Lord Salisbury (1830-1903)

164

I will call no being good, who is not what I mean when I apply that epithet to my fellow creatures; and if such a being can sentence me to hell for not so calling him, to hell I will go.

John Stuart Mill (1806-1873)

165

I was shown round Tutankhamun's tomb in the 1920s. I saw all this wonderful pink on the walls and the artefacts. I was so impressed that I vowed to wear it for the rest of my life.

Barbara Cartland (1901-2000)

166

There are three kinds of people: those who can count and those who can't.

167

Always be sincere, even if you don't mean it.

Harry S. Truman (1884-1972)

168

The man who has fed the chicken every day throughout its life, at last wrings its neck instead, showing that a more refined view as to the uniformity of nature would have been useful to the chicken.

Bertrand Russell (1872-1970)

169

When a Hyde Park heckler challenged Donald Soper (1903-1989), 'Is your name in the Lamb's Book of Life?' he replied, 'In it? It's on the cover!'

170

In reply to a heckler, Donald Soper said, 'The last thing I would want to be is reincarnated in an environment where I would encounter you all the time.' The heckler replied, 'That's what you said in your last reincarnation.'

171

Every time you wake up, you put in some practice for your own resurrection.

Rabbi Lionel Blue (b. 1930)

172

That's the way with these directors: they're always biting the hand that lays the golden egg.

Sam Goldwyn (1882-1974)

173

I have been an unconscionable time dying; I hope you will excuse it.

King Charles II (1630-1685)

174

Whistler has always spelt art with a capital 'I'.

Oscar Wilde (1854-1900)

175

We don't want pie in the sky when we die.
What we want is ham where we am.

176

A verbal contract isn't worth the paper it's written on.

Sam Goldwyn (1882-1974)

177

Every time I paint a portrait, I lose a friend.

John S. Sargent (1856-1925)

178

To err is human, but to really foul things up requires a computer.

179

Two monks on a journey have to ford a river swollen by rain. A young woman, frightened by the flood, asks for a lift, and the elder monk gives her a piggyback. The monks silently continue their journey, the younger one grumbling in his beard and finally bursting out angrily, 'How could you do something so shameless?' The elder replies, 'Brother, I left that woman three miles back by the riverside. You're still carrying her, aren't you!'

180

Why waste money on psychotherapy when you can listen to Bach's B Minor Mass?

Michael Torke (b. 1961)

181

The singers think they're going to be heard. It is the duty of the orchestra to make sure they are not.

Thomas Beecham (1879-1961)

182

I have recently been all round the world, and have formed a very poor opinion of it.

Thomas Beecham (1879-1961)

183

Why should people go out and pay to see bad movies when they can stay at home and see bad television for nothing?

Sam Goldwyn (1882-1974)

184

Greater love hath no man than this, that he lay down his friends for his life.

Jeremy Thorpe (b. 1929)

185

Englishmen will never be slaves: they are free to do whatever the government and public opinion allow them to do.

George Bernard Shaw (1856-1950)

186

An Englishman thinks he is moral when he is only uncomfortable.

George Bernard Shaw (1856-1950)

187

A cucumber should be well sliced, and dressed with pepper and vinegar, and then thrown out, as good for nothing.

Samuel Johnson (1709-1784)

188

I have always said it is a great mistake to prejudge the past.

William Whitelaw (1918-1999)

189

The Christian ideal has not been tried and found wanting. It has been found difficult, and left untried.

G. K. Chesterton (1874-1936)

190

On the whole, I'd rather be in Philadelphia.

Epitaph of W. C. Fields (1880-1946)

191

I often think how much easier the world would have been to manage if Herr Hitler and Signor Mussolini had been to Oxford.

Lord Halifax (1881-1959)

192

In theory, there is no difference between theory and practice, but in practice there is.

193

He who can, does. He who cannot, teaches.

George Bernard Shaw (1856-1950)

194

Education is what survives when what has been learned has been forgotten.

B. F. Skinner (1904-1990)

195

A woman's preaching is like a dog's walking on his hinder legs. It is not done well; but you are surprised to find it done at all.

Samuel Johnson (1709-1784)

196

Christmas is the Disneyfication of Christianity.

Don Cupitt (b. 1934)

197

I am frank about myself in this book. I tell of my first mistake on page 850.

Henry Kissinger (b. 1923)

198

There are two kinds of pedestrians: the quick and the dead.

George Robey (1869-1954)

199

Why do solipsists tout for membership of their Society?

200

God's revelation comes in two volumes: that of the Bible and that of Nature.

Thomas Aquinas (1225-1274)

201

On infallibility, the record of the Roman Church was extra-ordinarily good. It was consistent, and made no mistakes, largely because it had no thoughts.

Eamonn Duffy, 1998

202

The age of miracles is past. From now on, the only real miracles will be the changed lives of believers.

John Chrysostom (347-407)

203

If we make the mistake of thinking we are angels, we will become beasts.

Pascal (1623-1662)

204

Jesus did not say, 'I have come that they may have safety, and have it more abundantly'.

205

The major divisions (social, political, religious) are not between conservatives and liberals, but between those who think the world is simple, and those who know it is not.

206

The newspaper editor began his letter sacking his astrologer with the words, 'As you will already know . . .'

207

Europe spends fifty billion dollars a day on cigarettes. The entire world could have clean drinking water and sanitation for nine billion.

208

When Nancy Astor told Churchill that if she were his wife she would put poison in his coffee, he replied, 'And if I were your husband I would drink it.'

209

There is nothing so absurd but some philosopher has said it.

Cicero (106-43 BC)

210

If you're not part of the solution, you're part of the problem.

211

Almost everyone, when age,
Disease, or sorrows strike him,
Inclines to think there is a God,
Or something very like him.

A. H. Clough (1819-1861)

212

SMALL EARTHQUAKE IN CHILE. NOT MANY DEAD.

The Times, Dullest Headline Competition

213

He who begins by loving Christianity better than truth will proceed by loving his own sect or church better than Christianity, and end by loving himself better than all.

Samuel T. Coleridge (1772-1834)

214

Often when I pray, I wonder if I am not posting letters to a non-existent address.

C. S. Lewis (1898-1963)

215

The Iron Curtain did not reach the ground, and under it flowed liquid manure from the West.

Alexander Solzhenitsyn (b. 1918)

216

No one would remember the Good Samaritan if he'd only had good intentions. He had money as well.

Margaret Thatcher (b. 1925)

217

Bigotry tries to keep truth safe with a grip that kills it.

Rabindranath Tagore (1861-1941)

218

Freedom of the Press in Britain means freedom to print such of the proprietor's prejudices as the advertisers don't object to.

Hannen Swaffer (1879-1962)

219

Will the people in the cheaper seats clap your hands? All the rest of you, if you'll just rattle your jewellery.

John Lennon (1940-1980)

220

If we do not yet know about life, how can we know about death?

Confucius (551-479 BC)

221

The most serious charge which can be brought against New England is not Puritanism but February.

J. W. Krutch (1893-1970)

222

Discretion is not the better part of biography.

Lytton Strachey (1880-1932)

223

If you can keep your head when all around you are losing theirs, it's just possible you haven't grasped the situation.

Jean Kerr (b. 1923)

224

The difference between a wise man and a clever man is that the clever man will find a way of extricating himself out of a situation which the wise man would never have got into.

225

'Mummy, you know that vase you were always worried I might break? Well, your worries are over.'

226

God gave humans the power of speech so that they could hide their thoughts.

C. M. de Talleygrand-Périgord (1754-1838)

227

What the caterpillar calls the end, the rest of the world calls a butterfly.

Lao Tzu (604-531 BC)

228

You can make a throne out of bayonets, but you can't sit on it for long.

Boris Yeltsin (b. 1931)

229

'You seem to be in fine health,' said the doctor to the patient. 'But let's run a few tests; I'm sure we'll find something.'

230

On making the film *Titanic*: 'It would have been cheaper to lower the Atlantic.'

Lew Grade (1906-1998)

231

The real reason why the Tower of Babel was never completed is that the Ziggurat Committee could not agree whether the Mayor or the Macebearer should be the first person to set foot in heaven.

232

The only exercise I take is walking behind the coffins of friends who took exercise.

Mark Twain (1835-1910)

233

For her Desert Island discs, Elizabeth Schwartzkopf chose eight records of songs sung by herself.

234

When Max Baer was dying, he was asked whether he wanted the house doctor. 'No', he said. 'Get me a people doctor.'

235

When in Rome, look the other way when you're crossing the road.

236

Old age is not so bad when you consider the alternatives.

Maurice Chevalier (1888-1972)

237

The enemy of your enemy could be your enemy too.

238

Whenever I see a wall between Christians, I try to pull out a brick.

Pope John XXIII (1881-1963)

239

A sinner who has died comes before God seated on his Throne of Judgement. As the Recording Angel reads out page after page of the man's sins, God becomes uneasy and says, 'If I stay here and listen, I shall have to destroy this man.' So he gets up and moves to his Throne of Mercy.

Rabbinic

240

Man is the only animal that can remain on friendly terms with the victims he intends to eat until he eats them.

Samuel Butler (1835-1902)

241

Marriage is a wonderful invention; but, then again, so is a bicycle repair kit.

Billy Connolly (b. 1942)

242

Only those who do nothing make no mistakes.

Joseph Conrad (1857-1924)

243

A belief in a supernatural source of evil is not necessary; men alone are quite capable of every wickedness.

Joseph Conrad (1857-1924)

244

In dealing with non-Jews, be careful to be just as sincere with them as you are with Jews. In most places, Christians follow the same moral code as Jews.

Judah ben Samuel the Hasid (d. 1217)

245

There are no atheists in foxholes.

W. T. Cummings (1903-1945)

246

Flattery hurts no one, as long as he doesn't inhale.

Adlai Stevenson (1900-1965)

247

One death is a tragedy; a million deaths are only a statistic.

Joseph Stalin (1879-1953)

248

Your music is too beautiful for our ears. And far too many notes, dear Mozart.

Emperor Joseph II (1741-1790)

249

You campaign in poetry. You govern in prose.

Mario Cuomo (b. 1932)

250

Picasso is Spanish; so am I. Picasso is a genius; so am I. Picasso is known in every country in the world; so am I. Picasso is a Communist; I am not.

Salvador Dali (1904-1989)

251

Go and see the film, and you'll see for yourself why you shouldn't see it.

Sam Goldwyn (1882-1974)

252

Marriage is popular because it combines the maximum of temptation with the maximum of opportunity.

George Bernard Shaw (1856-1950)

253

Fortissimo at last!

Gustav Mahler (1860-1911) on seeing Niagara Falls

254

If voting changed anything, they'd abolish it.

Ken Livingstone (b. 1945)

255

No man but a blockhead ever wrote except for money.

Samuel Johnson (1709-1784)

256

I am monitoring party morale with the thermometer in my mouth, and I'm listening to it all the time.

William Whitelaw (1918-1999)

257

Democracy means government by the uneducated, while aristocracy means government by the badly educated.

G. K. Chesterton (1870-1936)

258

It's harder being fair to your family than to strangers: there's more expectation.

Rabbi Lionel Blue (b. 1930)

259

There is nothing behind my paintings, only the wall.

Rene Magritte (1898-1967)

260

During World War II, I consumed German wine with the excuse that I was not drinking it but interning it.

Winston Churchill (1874-1965)

261

The food in that restaurant is terrible. And such small portions.

Woody Allen (b. 1935)

262

A camel is a horse designed by a committee.

A. Issigonis (1906-1988)

263

Minds are like parachutes. They only function when they are open.

James Dewar (1842-1923)

264

If it turns out that there is a God, I don't think he's evil, just an under-achiever.

Woody Allen (b. 1935)

265

'Is it true that all things are relative?'
'Absolutely'

266

The dying Disraeli (1804-1881) was asked whether he would accept a visit from Queen Victoria. He replied, 'No, it is better not. She would only ask me to take a message to Albert!'

267

They'd been in the Folk Mass choir when they were in school but that, they knew now, hadn't really been singing . . . Real music was sex, and there wasn't much sex in 'Morning Has Broken' or 'The Lord Is My Shepherd'.

Roddy Doyle (b. 1958)

268

That sort of thing (homosexuality) may be tolerated by the French. But we're British, thank God.

Viscount Montgomery (1887-1926)

269

The best thing about the future is that it comes one day at a time.

Abraham Lincoln (1809-1865)

270

Reading one book is like eating one crisp.

Diane Duane (b. 1952)

271

Yesterday is history, and tomorrow is a mystery. But today is a gift: that's why we call it the present.

J. Walker

272

Science without religion is lame; religion without science is blind.

Albert Einstein (1879-1955)

273

When I was young, I found out that the big toe always ends up by making a hole in a sock. So I stopped wearing socks.

Albert Einstein (1879-1955)

274

When Conor Cruise O'Brien asked the Irish Civil Service to approve the admission of Hungarian refugees into Ireland as 'anti-Communists', he was told, 'We don't care what kind of Communists they are, we don't want them here.'

Conor Cruise O'Brien (b. 1917)

275

The sinking of the *Titanic* in 1912 was reported on the front page of the *Aberdeen Daily Journal* as ABERDEEN MAN LOST AT SEA.

276

If tobacco companies like Benson & Hedges are to be forbidden to advertise 'By Appointment to her Majesty the Queen', how will average citizens be able to die for their country?

277

When Noel Coward's name appeared on the Nazi list for extermination, he looked through the other names on the list and said, 'I wouldn't be seen dead with this lot.'

Noel Coward (1899-1973)

278

Humankind cannot bear very much reality.

T. S. Eliot (1888-1965)

279

'Twas God the Word that spake it,
He took the bread and brake it;
And what the word did make it,
That I believe and take it.

Queen Elizabeth I (1533-1603)

280

Blood sport is brought to its ultimate refinement in the gossip columns.

Bernard Ingham (b. 1932)

281

Several excuses are always less convincing than one.

Aldous Huxley (1894-1963)

282

I was never good at sightseeing, yet I suppose it has to be done.

William Wordsworth (1770-1850)

283

So God created man in his own image, in the image of God created he him; mail and e-mail created he them.

Genesis 1:27 (revised version)

284

What I'm really looking forward to is hindsight.

285

The Beatitudes contain a message that could save the world. What a pity that Christians have been listening to this message for two thousand years, but they're like stones lying in the water for centuries, never soaking up a single drop.

Mahatma Gandhi (1869-1948)

286

It was the nation that had the lion's heart. I had the luck to be called upon to give the roar.

Winston Churchill (1874-1965)

287

When I told Michelangelo I had paid Raphael far too much for that fresco, he told me the knee alone was worth it.

Giovanni Coricio (1512)

288

Do not seek for the City of God on earth, for it is not built of wood or stone; but seek it in the soul of those who are at peace with themselves.

Philo (20 BC-AD 40)

289

Here lies one whose name was writ in water.

John Keats (1795-1821), epitaph for his own tomb

290

It is not the voice but the choice,
Not the clarity but the charity,
not the harp but the heart,
that makes music in the ear of God.
Let your tongue reflect your thoughts,
and your thoughts be in tune with God. 1504.

Inscription in San Damiano, Assisi

291

There is no spectacle so ridiculous as the British public in one of its periodical fits of morality.

Thomas Macaulay (1800-1859)

292

When I address my God, I speak Spanish; my women, Italian; my men, French; and my horse, German.

Emperor Charles V (1500-1558)

293

When a man knows he is to be hanged in a fortnight, it concentrates his mind wonderfully.

Samuel Johnson (1709-1784)

294

A lapel badge reads: 'Nietzsche is dead. God'.

295

After God, Shakespeare created most.

Alexandre Dumas (1803-1870)

296

Politics are too serious a matter to be left to the politicians.

Charles de Gaulle (1890-1970)

297

Justice should not only be seen to be done, but to be actually done.

298

I know God will not give me anything I can't handle. I just wish he didn't trust me so much.

Mother Teresa of Calcutta (1910-1998)

299

When Einstein (1879-1955) was asked why he didn't keep a notebook to record his bright ideas, he replied that he'd only ever had one.

300

Serving God is doing good to others, but praying for them is thought an easier service, and therefore is more generally chosen.

Benjamin Franklin (1706-1790)

301

I can assure you that I might definitely take action.

William Whitelaw (1918-1999)

302

A notice in a Spanish hotel: 'If you are wishing to show feeling, wait till you see the manageress.'

303

The past is a foreign country: they do things differently there.

L. P. Hartley (1895-1972)

304

A single currency inevitable? It was inevitable the *Titanic* was going to set sail, but that doesn't mean it was a good idea to be on it.

William Hague (b. 1961)

305

The Bible tells us to forgive our enemies; it doesn't tell us to forgive our friends.

Cosimo de' Medici (1389-1464)

306

Once the toothpaste is out of the tube, it is awfully hard to get it back in.

H. R. Haldeman (1929-1993)

307

A secret in the Oxford sense is one that you may tell to only one person at a time.

Lord Franks (1905-1992)

308

Eternity is holding and possessing the whole fullness of life, past, present and to come, in one moment, here and now.

Boethius (476-524)

309

Anyone who says, 'I'll never surrender the right to control my own body' is like the caterpillar who says to the butterfly, 'You'll never catch me going up in one of those damned things.'

310

Having one child makes you a parent; having two makes you a referee.

David Frost (b. 1939)

311

May the road rise to meet you.
May the wind be always at your back.
May the sun shine warm upon your face,
and the rain fall soft upon your head.
And, until we meet again,
May God hold you in the palm of his hand.

Irish Blessing

312

Happiness makes up in height for what it lacks in length.

Robert Frost (1874-1963)

313

Any stigma will serve to beat a dogma.

Andrew Grove (b. 1936)

314

The best way to get rid of a temptation is to give in to it.

315

If you can actually count your money, then you're not really rich.

J. Paul Getty (1892-1976)

316

To be brave is to behave bravely when your heart is faint.
So you can be really brave only when you really ain't.

317

On first hearing bagpipes: 'I suppose one should be grateful that they don't also smell.'

318

O God, you must make your own some human word, because that's the only kind I can understand. Don't tell me everything that you are, don't tell me of your infinity – just tell me of your goodness to me . . . And please say it in *my* language, so I won't have to be afraid that the word 'love' hides some significance other than your goodness and gently mercy.

Karl Rahner (1904-1984)

319

Hope sees what is not, but yet will be.

320

It's better to wear out than to rust out.

Richard Cumberland (1631-1718)

321

Ask God to give thee skill in comfort's art,
That thou mayst consecrated be and set apart,
Into a life of sympathy.
For heavy is the weight of ill in every heart,
And comforters are needed much
Of Christlike touch.

A. E. Hamilton

322

My father was frightened of his mother; I was frightened
of my father, and I'm damned well going to see to it that
my children are frightened of me.

King George V (1965-1936)

323

How to become a millionaire? Start off as a billionaire and
then go into the airline business.

Richard Branson (b. 1945)

324

I don't know what art is, but I do know what it isn't.

Brian Sewell, 1999

325

Those who stand on their dignity will be left standing.

326

'What happens to boys who fail to get to university?'
'In later life, they tend to offer employment to those who did.'

An Ampleforth Headmaster

327

Forty years after publishing *Language, Truth and Logic*, in which he claimed that Logical Positivism had put an end to all philosophy, A. J. Ayer (1910-1989) was asked what were the faults in the book. He replied, 'Well, I suppose the most important defect was that nearly all of it was false.'

328

I cannot possibly vote Conservative while William Hague still leads the party. I hope he will accept there is nothing personal in this, and that it is purely on class grounds.

Auberon Waugh (b. 1939)

329

'Vote for insanity: you know it makes sense.'

Screaming Lord Sutch (1940-1999)

330

Shortly before he died, Screaming Lord Sutch (1940-1999) applied for permission to change his name to Margaret Thatcher by deed poll. He was refused because of the confusion it would cause at the next election.

331

Religion tells people to put up with misfortune.
Politics tells them to rebel against it.
Science finds a way of getting rid of it.

M. Perutz (b. 1914)

332

He (Wittgenstein) set out to circumcise logic; he all but
succeeded in castrating thought.

Arthur Koestler (1905-1983)

333

I believe in the sun even when it's not shining.
I believe in love even when I don't feel it.
I believe in God even when he is silent.

Jewish graffito in a Cologne cellar, 1946

334

Chastity without charity will be chained in hell.

William Langland (1330-1400)

335

Excess is a very good thing – in moderation.

336

In Mary's house the mourners gather:
Sorrow pierces them like a nail.
Where's Mary herself meanwhile?
Gone to comfort Judas's mother.

Norma Faber (1970)

337

Places where they burn books will end up by burning people.

Heinrich Heine (1797-1856)

338

Those who hear the message of the resurrection of Christ, and no longer hear the cry of the crucified contained in it, no longer hear the Gospel, but a myth.

Johann Metz (b. 1928)

339

What we can learn from history is that nobody has ever learnt anything from history, or acted upon the lessons it has taught us.

G. Hegel (1770-1831)

340

Never eat anything at one sitting that you can't lift.

Miss Piggy

341

The only sensible thing to do with bishops is to forgive them: a) because they need it more; and b) because it's the only way to show you're superior to them.

Albert Camus (1913-1960)

342

Cork is referred to as the Venice of Ireland, but who would ever dream of referring to Venice as the Cork of Italy?

343

The curate was deeply impressed by the preaching of a visiting monsignor, and enthused about it to his parish priest. The parish priest warned him to be cautious: 'At the last Judgement, St Peter will collect together all the simple priests and say, "Come in, my sons." But all monsignors, canons and bishops will be detained for further questioning.'

344

A statement made at the 1999 Conference of the Monster Raving Loony Party: 'We've been discussing the Homosexuality Bill, and decided to pay it.'

345

The Germans are the sort of people who would never storm a railway station unless they'd bought a platform ticket first.

Karl Marx (1818-1883)

346

Lord, if you're going to forgive me my trespasses as I forgive those who trespass against me, forget it.

347

All the people of God share in Christ's prophetic office. The entire body of the faithful cannot err in matters of belief. They manifest this special property of discerning matters of faith when, from bishops *down to* the last of the lay people, they show universal agreement in faith and morals.

Vatican II Decree, 'Lumen Gentium', Section 12

348

If you have a longstanding problem, try getting on your knees.

349

Asked about his acting abilities, Roger Moore said he had two: 'Left eyebrow raised, right eyebrow raised.'

350

'The Lord has sent me to tell you to stop smoking.'
'Tell the Lord, next time you see him, I don't like him talking about me behind my back.'

351

If you are unsure how popular you are, try to find out whether people who see you coming say 'Oh good' or 'Oh God'.

352

The really extraordinary thing about this institution we call the Church . . . is that without it we could know nothing about the Jesus whose message it so consistently compromises.

Bishop Holloway (b. 1933)

353

The Green Belt was a Labour idea, and we're going to build on it.

John Prescott, MP (b. 1938)

354

In the past, many people responded to the Church's *magisterium* out of fear. Today the fear has gone. So have the people.

355

If you want things to stay as they are, things will have to change.

G. di Lampedusa (1896-1957)

356

This book (*The Blind Watchmaker*) is written in the conviction that our own experience once presented the greatest of all mysteries, but that it is a mystery no longer because it is solved.

Richard Dawkins (b. 1941)

357

When George Eliot complimented the philosopher Herbert Spencer (1820-1903) on the lack of wrinkles on his forehead, he replied that nothing had ever really worried him.

358

Two wrongs are only a beginning.

359

I intend to live for ever. So far, so good.

360

All my wife has ever taken from the Mediterranean – from that whole vast intuitive culture – are four bottles of Chianti to make into table lamps.

Peter Schaffer (b. 1926)

361

The trouble with our generation is that we don't take humour seriously enough.

Konrad Lorenz, 1963

362

I'll give you a definite maybe.

Sam Goldwyn (1882-1974)

363

If a thing is worth doing, it is worth doing badly.

G. K. Chesterton (1874-1936)

364

Pagans are people who don't quarrel about religion.

365

A portrait is a painting with something wrong with the mouth.

J. S. Sargent (1856-1925)

366

Blood is thicker than water, and much more difficult to get out of the carpet.

Woody Allen (b. 1935)

367

When I was told that by the year 2100 women would rule the world, I replied, 'Still?'

Winston Churchill (1874-1965)

368

If you strike a child, take care that you strike it in anger, even at the risk of maiming it for life. A blow in cold blood neither can nor should be forgiven.

George Bernard Shaw (1856-1950)

369

It's a hard life being human, but it's interesting, and you don't die of boredom.

Rabbi Lionel Blue (b. 1930)

370

My eyes have seen what no one should witness: gas chambers built by learned engineers, children poisoned by educated physicians, infants killed by trained nurses, women and babies shot and burned by college graduates. So I am suspicious of education. Reading, writing and arithmetic are important only if they serve to make our children more human.

A survivor of the concentration camps

371

It is no small matter to stand up in the face of a congrega-
tion, and deliver a message of salvation or damnation, as
from the living God . . . I preached as never like to preach
again, and as a dying man to dying men.

Richard Baxter (1615-1691)

372

Science reassures; art is meant to disturb.

Georges Braque (1882-1963)

373

During the Council's discussion on what measures to take
after the recent floods, one councillor pointed out that the
water damage was secondary: far more urgent was the
fact that the whole sewage system was now seeping into
the floodwaters. In alarm, the Chairman announced,
'Well, of course, that is a completely different cup of tea.'

374

I am sympathetic to the 'no one is perfect' argument,
because it is obvious that anyone who wants to be a politi-
cian in the first place must automatically be a flawed
human being.

Sebastian Moore, OP

375

Lightning conductors were denounced as 'heretic rods' in
1752; trains in the 1820s and cars in the 1880s as sins
against nature; and air travel in the 1900s as an insult to
the Creator.

376

When the Russians liberated the concentration camp of Theresienstadt in 1945, they turned over the German guards to the inmates to do what they liked with them. Their rabbi, Leo Baeck (1873-1956) stopped the imminent slaughter, saying, 'Don't let the Nazis rob us of our decency', and demanded a fair trial.

377

A curious mixture of geniality and venom.

Churchill's description of Herbert Morrison (1888-1965)

378

As the Duke of Edinburgh stepped off the plane, an airport official asked,
'And how was your flight, Sir?'
'Have *you* ever flown?'
'O yes, Sir, many times.'
'Well, it was like that.'

379

O! Mankinde,
Have in thy minde
My passion smart;
And thou shalt finde
Me full kinde.
Lo! Here my heart.

Anon (15th century)

380

When Albino Luciani was elected pope in 1978, he was acclaimed by Cardinal Hume (1923-1999) as 'God's Own Candidate'. The pope died 33 days later.

381

After a meeting attended by Denis Healy, his wife Edna told him, 'We can go now, Denis. I don't think there's anyone else you haven't insulted.'

382

A passer-by congratulated the gardener on his co-operation with God to create a beautiful garden. He replied, 'Well, you should have seen it when God had it all to himself.'

383

I am glad I was able to keep my vow of celibacy. If I hadn't, it might have been used as an argument for the apostolic authorship of the Fourth Gospel, or the Mosaic authorship of the Pentateuch.

Alfred Loisy (1857-1940) after his 1908 excommunication

384

Do not attach yourself exclusively to any particular creed in such a way that you reject the rest. You would lose much that is good, and fail to see the truth. No single creed can capture God.

Ibn el Arabi (13th century)

385

We dream in narrative, daydream in narrative, remember, anticipate, hope, despair, believe, doubt, plan, revise, criticise, construct, gossip, learn, hate and love by narrative.

Brian Wicker

386

The only power God has in the world is the love he inspires in us.

Simone Weil (1909-1943)

387

Don't listen to those who keep saying the voice of the people is the voice of God. A rioting crowd is always close to madness.

Alcuin (735-804)

388

All music is folk music. I ain't ever heard no horse sing.

Louis Armstrong (1901-1971)

389

When a philosopher told Alexander the Great that there could be an infinite number of worlds, he burst into tears: 'I haven't even got this one under control yet!'

Alexander the Great (356-323 BC)

390

It's not that I'm afraid to die. I just don't want to be there when it happens.

Woody Allen (b. 1935)

391

Nobody likes having salt rubbed into their wounds, even if it is the salt of the earth.

Rebecca West (1892-1983)

392

Barbarism is a permanent and universal human characteristic, which becomes more or less pronounced according to circumstances.

Simone Weil (1909-1943)

393

Christ has no body on earth but yours, no hands but yours, no feet but yours.

Teresa of Avila (1515-1582)

394

You have no idea how much nastier I would be if I was not a Catholic. Without supernatural aid I would hardly be a human being.

Evelyn Waugh (1903-1966)

395

A Church that can feel as its own all that is human, and wants to incarnate the pain, the hope, the affliction of all who suffer and feel joy, such a Church will be Christ loved and awaited, Christ present.

Oscar Romero (1917-1980)

396

When he told a lady how ugly she was, and she retorted by telling him how drunk he was, Churchill concluded, 'Yes madam, but tomorrow I will be sober.'

Winston Churchill (1874-1965)

397

You are blessed who are gentle and meek,
For the war-cries of rage are the tunes of the weak:
Your silence is long,
And the trumpets of anger blow strong;
But the Kingdom will dance to your song.

Malcolm Stewart (b. 1938)

398

No one listens until you make a mistake.

399

You'll hear it said that God is dead,
Two thousand years ago they said it too –
It's nothing new,
Two thousand years this has been true.
Today the only stone that rolls away to let him live
Is inside you.

Malcolm Stewart (b. 1938)

400

Great Britain found it easier to conquer the East than to
know what to do with it.

Horace Walpole (1717-1797)

401

They (the clergy) seem to know no medium between a
mitre and a crown of martyrdom. One would think their
motto was 'Canterbury or Smithfield'.

Horace Walpole (1717-1797)

402

Common sense is not as common as all that.

Voltaire (1694-1798)

403

There are two golden rules for an orchestra: start together and finish together. The public doesn't give a damn what goes on in between.

Thomas Beecham (1879-1961)

404

Ronald Reagan – a triumph of the embalmer's art.

Gore Vidal (b. 1925)

405

Silence is a woman's finest ornament.

Aristotle (384-322 BC)

406

She's the sort of woman who lives for others. You can always tell the others by their hunted expression.

C. S. Lewis (1898-1963)

407

Silence is the virtue of fools.

Francis Bacon (1561-1626)

408

When Cardinal Bellarmine (1542-1621) published his Catechism in 1605, he was asked why he had omitted the Eight Beatitudes. He replied, 'Nobody can remember more than seven of anything.'

409

Too many people forget about generosity when they're practising charity.

Albert Camus (1930-1960)

410

Liberty is liberty, not equality, or fairness, or justice, or human happiness, or a quiet conscience.

Isaiah Berlin (1909-1997)

411

The war situation has developed not necessarily to Japan's advantage.

Emperor Hirohito announcing Japan's surrender in August 1945

412

There's no better way of exercising the imagination than the study of law. No poet ever interpreted nature as freely as a lawyer interprets the truth.

Jean Giraudoux (1882-1944)

413

I read the newspapers avidly. It is my one form of continuous fiction.

Aneurin Bevan (1897-1960)

414

If you open that Pandora's Box, you never know what Trojan horses will jump out.

Ernest Bevin (1881-1951)

415

Obedience keeps the rules. Love knows when to break them.

Zen saying

416

Charlemagne (747-814), founder of the 'Holy Roman Empire', divorced his first wife, had six children by the second, two by the third, and at least one child by each of his twelve concubines. Historians concede that he was always a considerate father.

417

All I ask is a chance to prove that money can't make me happy.

Spike Milligan (b. 1918)

418

If I had known I was going to live so long, I'd have taken better care of myself.

George Burns (1896-1996)

419

God grant me the senility to forget the people I never liked anyway, the good fortune to run into the ones I did like, and the eyesight to tell the difference.

Terry Wogan (b. 1938)

420

There was a young lady of Slough,
Who last week developed a cough:
She wasn't to know
It would last until now,
But hopes that by next week it's through.

421

It is better to entertain an idea than to take it home to live with you for the rest of your life.

R. Jarrell (1914-1965)

422

Johann Tetzel, OP (1465-1519), chief fund-raiser for the building of St Peter's in Rome, offered an 'indulgence' so potent that it would even remit the sin of someone who had raped the Virgin Mary.

423

A feast day is holy because it shows that all days of the year are holy.
A sanctuary is holy because it shows that all places are the dwelling place of God.
Jesus was born to show that all people are the sons and daughters of God.

Anthony de Mello, SJ (1931-1987)

424

'All those people here who believe in telekinesis, raise my hand!'

425

My belief gets some support from the Scriptures, but not as much as I want. They strike me as a mix of what actually happened, what people wanted to happen, and what people thought was the meaning of what happened. I still can't unscramble them.

Rabbi Lionel Blue (b. 1930)

426

This boy shows great originality, which must be crushed at all costs.

A school report of Peter Ustinov (b. 1921)

427

Even reason is a matter of faith. It is an act of faith to assert that our thoughts have any relationship to reality at all.

G. K. Chesterton (1874-1936)

428

The Tory party does not like brains; thank God I don't have any.

William Whitelaw (1918-1999)

429

I don't blame anyone except perhaps all of us.

William Whitelaw (1918-1999)

430

Ought we perhaps to read:
Blessed are those who are rich,
for they will inherit the earth?
Blessed are the famous,
for they will enjoy the praise of men?
Blessed are the mighty,
for they will become more powerful yet?

George Carey, Archbishop of Canterbury (b. 1935)

431

The longer I live, the more I see that I am never wrong about anything, and that all the pains I have so humbly taken to verify my notions have only wasted my time.

George Bernard Shaw (1856-1950)

432

The change in the world that you're longing for starts with you.

Mahatma Gandhi (1869-1948)

433

I don't like abroad. I've been there.

King George V (1865-1936)

434

Only a rose is fragile enough to express eternity.

Paul Claudel (1868-1955)

435

Dancing is a perpendicular expression of a horizontal desire.

George Bernard Shaw (1856-1950)

436

Remember, Fathers, that when you die, someone will be relieved.

Cardinal Basil Hume (1923-1999) addressing his clergy

437

I did not hear the honourable gentleman's question. If I did, the answer would be yes. As I didn't, the answer is no.

William Whitelaw (1918-1999)

438

My whole life has been a downhill struggle.

439

How to make crime pay: become a lawyer.

440

Far too many cooks spoil the broth.

441

I can't listen to that much Wagner. I start getting the urge to conquer Poland.

Woody Allen (b. 1935)

442

Having your book turned into a film is like seeing your oxen turned into Oxo cubes.

John Le Carré (b. 1931)

443

Asked about the one luxury item that he would take to his Desert Island, Robert Mark opted for a TV set that doesn't work.

444

Heard on the golf green: 'Daddy, why musn't the ball go into the little hole?'

445

I would far rather feel remorse than know how to define it.

Thomas à Kempis (1380-1471)

446

When I can see no other way of teaching a well-established truth except by pleasing one intelligent man and displeasing ten thousand fools, I prefer to address myself to the one man.

Maimonides (1135-1204)

447

In 1969 I published a small book on humility. It was a pioneering work which has not, to my knowledge, been superseded.

Lord Longford (b. 1905)

448

I always like to associate with a lot of priests because it makes me understand anticlericals.

449

The awe and dread with which the untutored savage contemplates his mother-in-law are amongst the most familiar facts of anthropology.

James G. Frazer (1854-1941)

450

Outside of a dog, a book is a man's best friend. Inside a dog, it's too dark to read.

Groucho Marx (1895-1977)

451

The great advantage of an English public school is that no subsequent form of captivity can hold any particular terror for you.

John Mortimer (b. 1923)

452

82.6 per cent of statistics are made up on the spot.

453

Sir, I have found you an argument; but I am not obliged to find you an understanding.

Samuel Johnson (1709-1784)

454

A problem shared is called gossip.

455

Dear Lord, if there is cricket in heaven, let there also be rain.

Alec Douglas-Home (1903-1995)

456

Clothes make the man. Naked people have little or no influence on society.

Mark Twain (1835-1910)

457

An anthropologist asked a Red Indian what his people called America before the white man came. He replied, 'Ours.'

458

On entering America, Gilbert Harding had to fill in an Immigration Authority form asking, 'Is it your intention to overthrow the US government by force?' He wrote, 'Sole purpose of visit.'

459

From the earliest times, the old have rubbed it into the young that they are wiser than they. And before the young had discovered what nonsense this was, they were old too, and it profited them to carry on the imposture.

W. Somerset Maugham (1874-1965)

460

On the continent people have good food. In England people have good table manners.

George Mikes (b. 1912)

461

An alcoholic is a man you don't like who drinks as much as you do.

Dylan Thomas (1914-1953)

462

Original writers are not those who refrain from imitating others, but those whom none can imitate.

Chateaubriand (1768-1848)

463

Better authentic mammon than a bogus god.

Louis MacNeice (1907-1963)

464

Love your neighbour, but don't pull down the fence.

Chinese proverb

465

I have the greatest admiration for people who can take private revelation on board. It's taken me all my lifetime to take on board the public revelation in Galilee two thousand years ago.

Bishop C. Butler (1902-1982)

466

The poor have to work under the majestic equality of the law, according to which sleeping under bridges, begging in the streets and stealing bread is forbidden to both the rich and the poor.

Anatole France (1844-1924)

467

Winning is everything. The only ones who remember you when you come second are your wife and your dog.

Damon Hill (b. 1960)

468

Would men ever have embarked on the Crusades if their overriding image of God had been of a mother caring for her young?

Bruce Deakin

469

In the two years after the death of Eva Peron in 1952, the Vatican received 40,000 letters reporting miracle cures through her intercession.

470

At a photocall in 1999, Margaret Thatcher told Ted Heath that he should be on her right. 'That would be difficult' he replied.

471

Women are versatile, tough and contain within their variability all that falls within the range of the normal. Men are freaks of nature, frail, fantastic, bizarre.

Germaine Greer (b. 1939)

472

He that lives upon hope will die fasting.

Benjamin Franklin (1706-1790)

473

When he was asked what was the use of a new invention, Benjamin Franklin replied: 'What is the use of a new-born child?'

Benjamin Franklin (1706-1790)

474

Thanks to the millennium, the fireworks industry is experiencing an explosion.

Fireworks Director, December 1999

475

Millions long for immortality who don't know what to do with themselves on a rainy Sunday afternoon.

Susan Ertz (1894-1985)

476

January Snowy, February Flowy, March Blowy,
April Showery, May Flowery, June Bowery,
July Hoppy, August Croppy, September Droppy,
October Breezy, November Sneezy, December Freezy.

George Ellis (1753-1815)

477

Space isn't remote at all. It's only an hour's drive away if
your car could go straight upwards.

Fred Hoyle (b. 1915)

478

No poetry can delight or endure for long
That's written by those who drink water.

Horace (65-8 BC)

479

You can drive out nature with a pitchfork, but it will
always come running back.

Horace (65-8 BC)

480

No warmth, no cheerfulness, no healthful ease,
No comfortable feel in any member –
No shade, no shine, no butterflies, no bees,
No fruits, no flowers, no leaves, no birds –
November!

Thomas Hood (1799-1845)

481

The sense of being well dressed gives a feeling of inward tranquillity which religion is powerless to bestow.

C. F. Forbes (1817-1911)

482

Beauty is in the eye of the beer-holder.

483

He (John Wyclif, 1329-1384) has turned the Gospel, which Christ gave to the clergy, into something vulgar. The Gospel pearl has been scattered abroad, and is being trodden underfoot by swine.

14th-century book review

484

The early bird may get the worm, but it's the second mouse that gets the cheese.

485

Harold Wilson is going round the country, stirring up apathy.

William Whitelaw (1918-1999)

486

Life is something to do when you can't get to sleep.

Fran Lebowitz (b. 1946)

487

A man who has not been to Italy is always conscious of an inferiority.

Samuel Johnson (1709-1784)

488

When a man is tired of London, he is tired of life.

Samuel Johnson (1709-1784)

489

It is sobering to consider that when Mozart was my age, he had already been dead a year.

Tom Lehrer (b. 1928)

490

A group of teachers in 1999, protesting against the increasingly frequent testing of children, have suggested that it is apparently more important to weigh children than to feed them.

491

Ideals are dangerous things. Realities are better. They wound, but they're better.

Oscar Wilde (1854-1900)

492

My country is the world, and my religion is to do good.

Thomas Paine (1737-1809)

493

Whereof one cannot speak, thereof one must be silent.

Ludwig Wittgenstein (1889-1951)

494

The ideal reader of my novels is a lapsed Catholic and a failed musician, short-sighted, colour-blind, auditorily biased, who has read the books that I have read. He should also be about my age.

Anthony Burgess (1917-1993)

495

Love does not consist in gazing at each other, but in looking together in the same direction.

Antoine de St Exupéry (1900-1944)

496

The pidgin-English for a helicopter is 'Mixmaster him belong Jesus Christ.'

497

It is with the heart that one sees rightly; what is essential is invisible to the eye.

Antoine de St Exupéry (1900-1944)

498

A newspaper reporter sent a telegram to Cary Grant asking, HOW OLD CARY GRANT? He replied, OLD CARY GRANT FINE, HOW YOU?

499

Monarchy is like something kept behind a curtain, about which there is a great deal of bustle and fuss, and a wonderful air of seeming solemnity; but when, by any accident, the curtain happens to be open, and the company see what it is, they burst into laughter.

Thomas Paine (1737-1809)

500

What if there had been Three Wise Women instead of Three Wise men? They would have:
1. asked for directions;
2. been on time;
3. helped deliver the baby;
4. brought practical gifts;
5. cleaned the stable;
6. made a casserole.

Letter to the 'Independent', December 1999

INDEX